Giant Kangaroo
(Protemnodon viator)
Up to 2m tall
Lord Howe Island
Horned Turtle
(Meiolania platyceps)
Up to 2m long
Giant Short-Faced
Kangaroo
(Procoptodon goliah)
Up to 3m tall
Diprotodon
(Diprotodon optatum)
2m tall, 4m long
Giant Malleefowl
(Progura gallinacea)
Weighed up to 8kg
Megalania
(Varanus priscus)
Up to 6m long
Bluff Downs
Giant Python
(Liasis dubudingala)
Up to 10m long

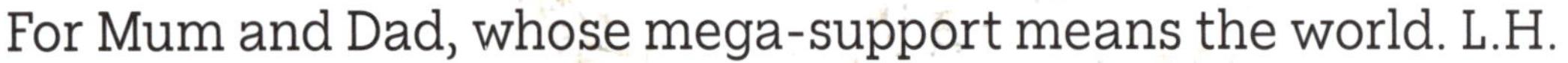

For Mum and Dad, whose mega-support means the world. L.H.

For Lila, Iris and Neve, Simon and Mum. L.D.

Wild Dog Books would like to thank Vikram Neelesh Vakil for his careful and thorough fact checking. Vikram is currently completing his PhD in Vertebrate Palaeontology at the University of Queensland.

First published in 2025 by
wild dog
Melbourne, Australia
wdog.com.au

ISBN: 9 781 7420368 30

A catalogue record for this book is available from the National Library of Australia

Printed and bound in China by
Everbest Printing Investment Limited

10 9 8 7 6 5 4 3 2 1 25 26 27 28 29 30

FSC® is a non-profit international organisation established to promote the responsible management of the world's forests.

Laura Holloway
illustrated by
Liz Duthie
MEGA!
AUSTRALIA'S MEGAFAUNA
wild dog

A long, long time ago

Australia looked very different.

We're talking 2.5 million –
11,700 years ago, known as the Pleistocene Epoch.

Sea levels were lower, meaning Tasmania, Papua New Guinea, and the Torres Strait Islands were attached to the mainland. Together with the Indonesian Aru Islands, they formed an ancient landmass, known as Sahul, which was around 30% bigger than Australia is today.

The landscapes and climates were very different.

Sea levels were
lower so you
could walk acros
here
RAINFOREST
WOODLANDS
GRASSLANDS
DESERT
Pleistocene Australia
Tasmania
was attached

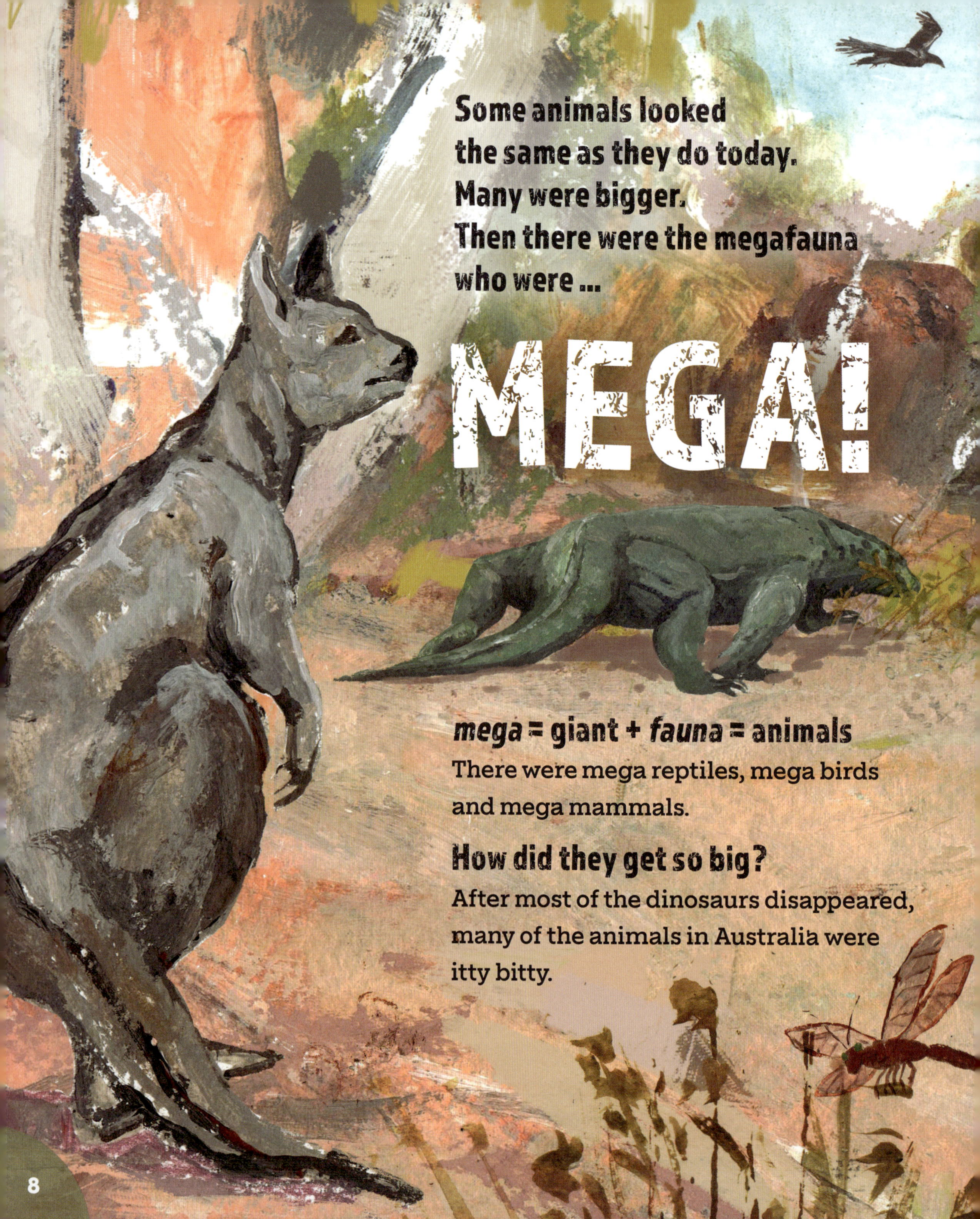

Some animals looked the same as they do today. Many were bigger. Then there were the megafauna who were ...

MEGA!

mega = giant + _fauna_ = animals

There were mega reptiles, mega birds and mega mammals.

How did they get so big?

After most of the dinosaurs disappeared, many of the animals in Australia were itty bitty.

Some species gradually grew bigger,
filling the gap left by the dinosaurs and moving up the food chain.
The megafauna had a motto – the bigger you are, the harder you are to eat!

There is no exact definition of 'megafauna'. Generally, it's animals over 45kg. Other definitions include any animal larger than a human, or any animal that is significantly larger than today's version.

Geological Time Scale

EARTH FORMED

• 4.6 billion years ago

PRECAMBRIAN SUPEREON

• Billions and billions of years pass (This line is FAR TOO LONG to draw!)

CAMBRIAN EXPLOSION

• 541 million years ago
• First fish: 530 million years ago
• First amphibians: 370 million years ago
• First reptiles: 315 million years ago

Australia is still connected to Antarctica via Tasmania

BYE BYE DINOSAURS!

• An asteroid destroyed most of them around 66 million years ago

CENOZOIC ERA

• 66 million years ago – present

First monotremes

• 130 million years ago

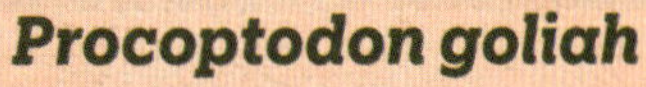

Procoptodon goliah

• 2.5 million – 15,000 years ago

Diprotodon optatum

• 2.5 million – 25,000 years ago

Permian pelycosaur
(proto-mammal)
Dinosaurs
Permian Extinction
• Destroys 90% of species on Earth
252 million years ago
Pangaea splits into Gondwana and Laurasia
• Approximately
200 million years ago
PALAEOZOIC ERA
• 538 – 252 million years ago
• All continents connected in one land mass, Pangaea
Mega continent Gondwana
starts to break up circa 180 million years ago
MESOZOIC ERA
• 252 – 66 million years ago
Jurassic dinosaur
PLEISTOCENE EPOCH
• The heyday of the MEGAFAUNA
• 2.5 million – 11,700 years ago
Humans arrived
on the continent at least 50,000 years ago
Many animals have become extinct
We are here
Genyornis newtoni
• Lived during the Pleistocene Epoch
• Could have lived alongside humans

Newton's Thunder Bird

(Genyornis newtoni)

Sahul was home to the thunder birds, nicknamed 'demon ducks of doom'! They could not fly but were surprisingly fast runners thanks to their strong legs and feet. They were related to ducks and geese, but strangely not emus. The last species of thunder bird, *Genyornis*, was over 2m tall. Ancient rock paintings suggest *Genyornis* may have become tasty dinners for First Nations people.

Newton's Thunder Bird had an even bigger relative that lived during the late Miocene Epoch (11 – 5 million years ago). Stirton's Thunder Bird (Dromornis stirtoni) was 500kg and 3m tall!

Giant Malleefowl

(Progura gallinacea)

Nicknamed the 'tall turkey', the giant malleefowl weighed up to 8kg – more than 4 times the weight of its living brush turkey relatives. Unlike many big birds, it could fly and roosted in trees. Most fossils have been found in underground caves as the malleefowl had a bad habit of falling in.

It was part of the Megapode family.

mega = giant + *pode* = feet

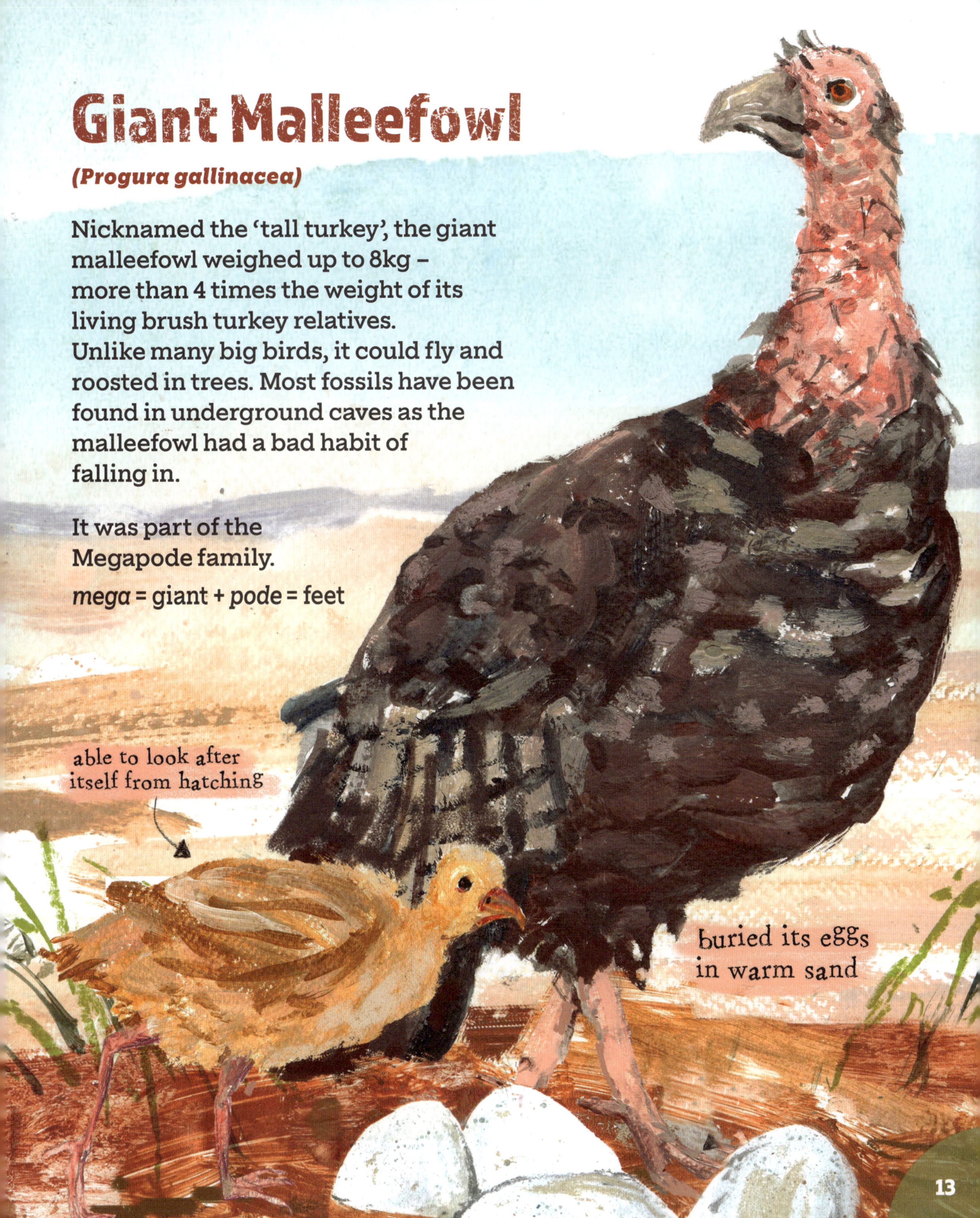

An extremely large snake features in many Dreaming stories from different First Nations groups across Australia. Often referred to as the Rainbow Serpent in English, the name and story vary across regions. The 5m Wonambi python was named after a Central Australian Aboriginal term for the Rainbow Serpent of the Dreaming.

Bluff Downs Giant Python

(Liasis dubudingala)

At 10m long, the Bluff Downs Giant Python was Australia's longest snake ever. Like all snakes, the giant python was a cold-blooded carnivore who swallowed its food whole.

It lived 4 million years ago – before the Pleistocene – and scientists have pieced together what is known about this super snake from only a few back bones, rib fragments and a piece of its skull.

Lord Howe Island Horned Turtle

(Meiolania platyceps)

The *Meiolania* was twice the size of the biggest turtle around today – the Galapagos giant tortoise. It had a hard shell, horned head and spiked tail for protection. While these features made the turtle hard to chomp on, the horns meant its head wouldn't have fit in its shell. Despite its mega size, its name means 'little roamer' in Greek. This is because its fossils were first thought to be a smaller version of the giant lizard, megalania.

Quinkana

(Quinkana fortirostrum)

Unlike most crocodiles, which are aquatic, the quinkana lived on land. It was a fast runner, which helped it chase down mammals, birds and reptiles for dinner. While modern crocs grip prey in their jaws and drown it underwater, land-dwelling quinkana had sharp, blade-like teeth to chop unlucky animals into pieces before eating.

largest venomous
animal – ever!
cold-blooded
name means
'great roamer'
in Greek

Megalania

(Varanus priscus)

You would not want to come face-to-face with this giant! The biggest lizard ever, megalania was the size of a saltwater croc at up to 6m long. It had toxic saliva, sharp claws, serrated teeth and a powerful tail it may have used like a whip. Osteoderms, a layer of bony armour, protected its skin. It is related to Komodo dragons, who no longer live in Australia but are believed to have evolved here.

Hackett's Giant Echidna

(Murrayglossus hacketti)

The giant echidna was similar to the modern long-beaked echidnas found in New Guinea but was about the size of a large dog. It had sharp claws for digging and a long sticky tongue to help catch termites, beetles, grubs and worms. A spiny body and the ability to roll up into a ball helped keep it off the carnivore menu.

Riversleigh Platypus

(Obdurodon dicksoni)

The Riversleigh platypus was around twice as long and 4 times heavier than its modern relatives. It had an amphibious lifestyle, spending time on land and in fresh water. While the modern platypus is toothless as an adult, the Riversleigh platypus had large teeth. It would have snacked on insect larvae, frogs, fish and yabbies.

The platypus is a uniquely Aussie icon, but the fossilised tooth of an ancient relative of the platypus was recently found in Patagonia, Argentina. This proves that platypus ancestors were around when Australia and South America formed part of the supercontinent Gondwana, at least 180 million years ago.

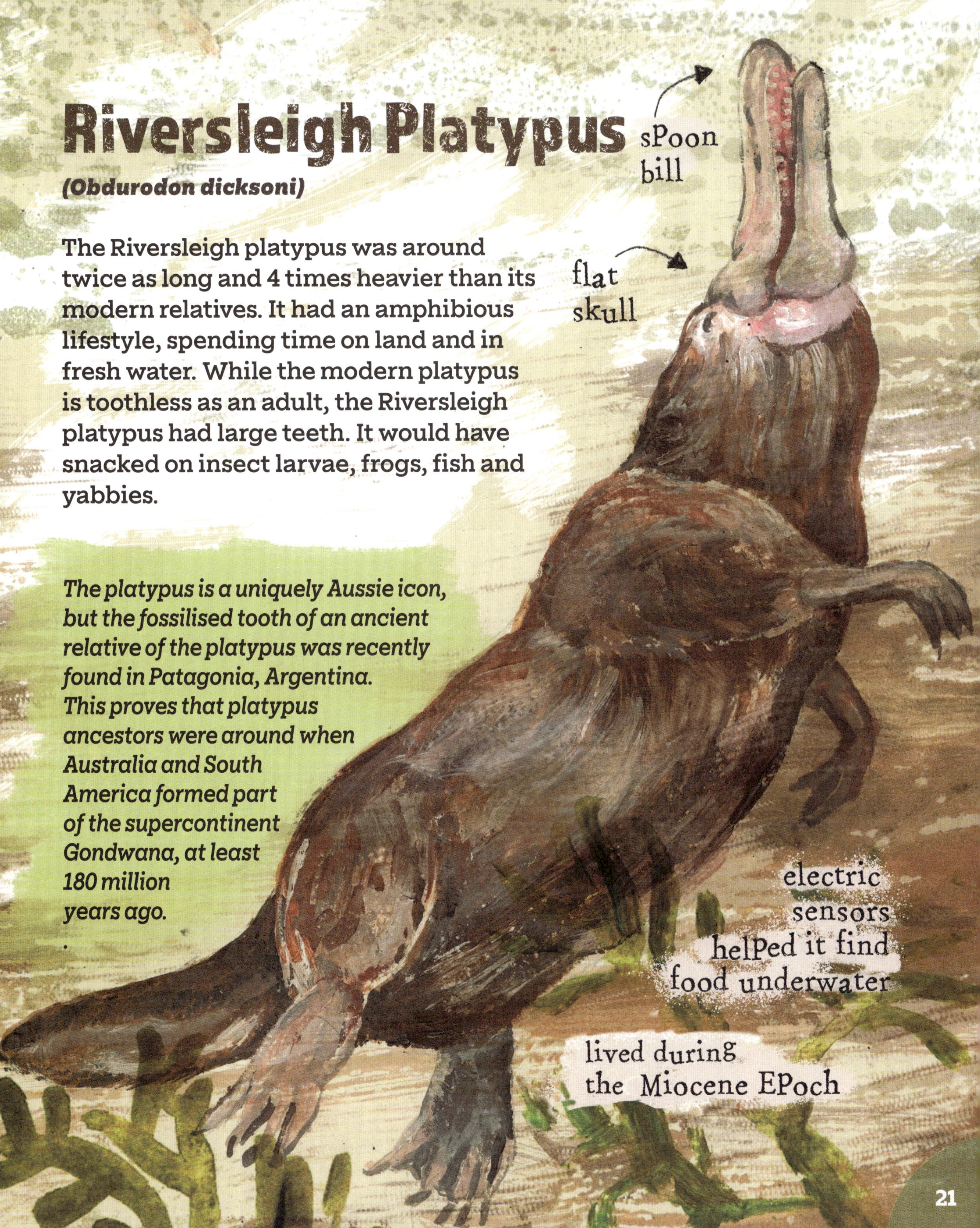

body like a wombat
ate 100–150kg
of vegetation
each day
pouch
small feet
strong claws

Diprotodon

(Diprotodon optatum)

The biggest Aussie megafauna of all* was diprotodon. It was a marsupial with a pouch and a relative of both koalas and wombats. One diprotodon would have weighed nearly 3000kg and measured 4m long! Although huge, it was a herbivore who only ate shrubs and trees. Diprotodon got its name from its two front teeth which never stopped growing.

*as far as we know!

While several diprotodon skulls have been found, scientists can't be sure whether it had a small trunk or not because soft tissue usually decays quickly when an animal dies:

Marsupial Pygmy Hippopotamus

(Zygomaturus trilobus)

Despite living in swamps and feasting on reeds and other greens like a modern-day hippo, the marsupial pygmy hippopotamus was not really a hippo at all. It was actually a large marsupial and a member of the Diprotodontidae family. It used its tusk-like teeth and claws to rip up whole plants.

Marsupial Tapir

(Palorchestes azael)

The marsupial tapir was another member of the Diprotodontidae family, weighing in at around 1000kg and measuring 2m long.

Unlike its cousins, it lived in forests and had strong arms, curved claws and a long, thin tongue to help it rip branches and bark off trees. Its scientific name, *Palorchestes*, is a case of mistaken identity – its fossils were originally thought to be a kangaroo, so 'ancient leaper' was chosen.

Marsupial Lion

(Thylacoleo carnifex)

Another megafauna with a misleading nickname is the marsupial lion, which was a marsupial but was absolutely not a lion. *Thylacoleo* was a ferocious hunter with hooked claws and a combination of slicing and stabbing teeth. It is believed that the marsupial lion had the strongest bite of any mammal – living or extinct!

It wasn't a very fast runner, so probably ambushed rather than chased its prey. Scratch marks found in a cave in Western Australia have led scientists to believe *Thylacoleo* raised its young in communal caves.

Giant Short-Faced Kangaroo

(Procoptodon goliah)

The largest species of kangaroo ever, *Procoptodon goliah*, could have touched the ceiling in most homes. It had a short, flat face and eyes that faced forward. This mega roo had long arms and flexible shoulders, allowing it to reach high branches to snack on. Unlike smaller kangaroos, the giant short-faced kangaroo walked rather than hopped.

Procoptodon was a genus of sthenurine kangaroo which lived on Sahul during the Pleistocene Epoch. Scientists don't know why sthenurines didn't survive past the Pleistocene when other kangaroo species did.

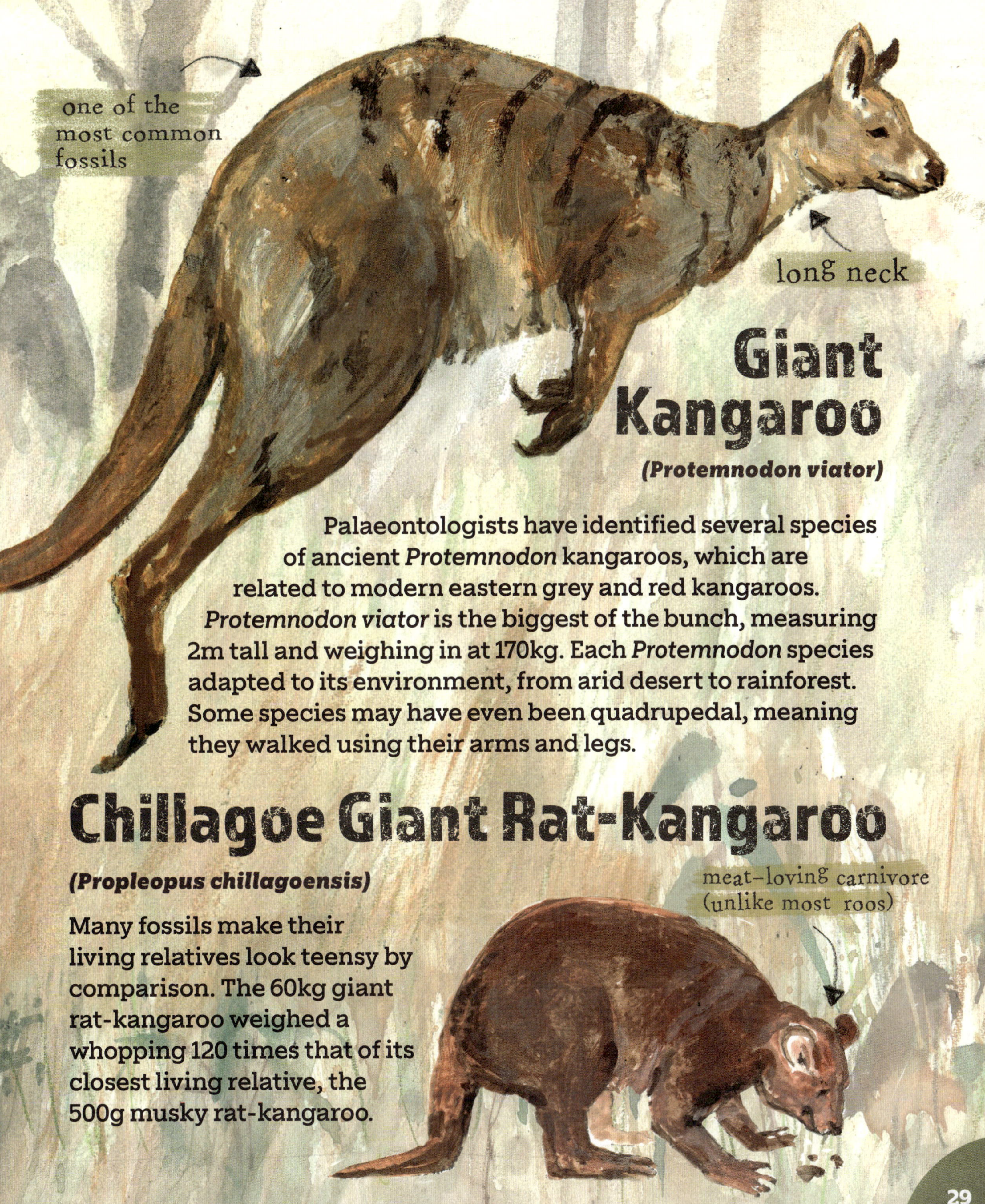

Giant Kangaroo

(Protemnodon viator)

Palaeontologists have identified several species of ancient *Protemnodon* kangaroos, which are related to modern eastern grey and red kangaroos. *Protemnodon viator* is the biggest of the bunch, measuring 2m tall and weighing in at 170kg. Each *Protemnodon* species adapted to its environment, from arid desert to rainforest. Some species may have even been quadrupedal, meaning they walked using their arms and legs.

Chillagoe Giant Rat-Kangaroo

(Propleopus chillagoensis)

Many fossils make their living relatives look teensy by comparison. The 60kg giant rat-kangaroo weighed a whopping 120 times that of its closest living relative, the 500g musky rat-kangaroo.

Living with Giants

Evidence found in Arnhem Land in the Northern Territory tells us that First Nations people arrived in Sahul at least 50,000 years ago, during the Pleistocene Epoch. This suggests that humans and some megafauna were neighbours for tens of thousands of years.

Many First Nations stories, passed down through hundreds of generations, feature oversized animals such as snakes, birds and kangaroos. Could some of these stories actually be based on eyewitness accounts?

Another place megafauna seem to show up is in ancient art. Studies of rock art in Arnhem Land have identified details that may indicate that paintings once thought to show modern animals and spiritual creatures instead show megafauna including *Genyornis*, *Thylacoleo*, *Palorchestes* and *Procoptodon*.

Digging up Evidence

Is there fossil evidence? Well, sort of.

- The burnt shells of thunder bird eggs have been found, suggesting they were cooked by humans.

- Diprotodon bones were discovered at the Warratyi rock shelter in the Flinders Ranges, South Australia. The climb was too steep for a diprotodon. Could it have been carried there by humans?

- Evidence from the Cuddie Springs archaeological and palaeontological site in New South Wales shows humans and megafauna living there in the same time period.

The conditions for preserving fossils are rare, and finding the evidence thousands of years later is even rarer. Scientists are working towards dating various fossils to try to put humans and megafauna in the same place at the same time, but it's hard to be sure.

Fossils

When it comes to fossils, most people picture bones. However, fossils come in plenty of other forms:

- teeth, shells and eggshells
- footprints or trackways
- scratch marks
- fossilised poop
- fossilised plants
- microfossils such as pollen and algae
- fossil impressions – this means the organic matter is no longer there, but a gap left behind shows what was once there
- soft tissue fossils – it's rare, but soft tissue can be fossilised in amber or preserved in ice

Palaeo – what?

Fossils tell the megafauna story. To understand the past, scientists called palaeontologists piece together information like a puzzle. Fossils can be used to identify extinct species, figure out information about breeding, diet and lifestyles, or paint a picture of what an area was like in the past, including the climate, landscape and which plants were around. As more fossils are discovered, what is known about megafauna will change.

Very few fossil specimens have been found for some megafauna species, so even one new fossil could drastically change what we think we know!

Today, most Aussie megafauna have either shrunk or disappeared. Scientists aren't sure why, but they have a few theories.

Were they hunted by humans?

When humans arrive in new places, extinctions often occur. Hunting of animals, introducing new species, land clearing and other human activities can all have serious consequences for unsuspecting animals. It's true that within a few thousand years of humans arriving in Sahul, much of the megafauna had disappeared, but there isn't any conclusive evidence that humans were the cause.

Were they hit by an asteroid?

That's how the dinosaurs were wiped out, but it doesn't seem to be the case for the megafauna.

Was climate change the cause?

Changing conditions at the end of the Great Ice Age could have threatened the megafauna. As the climate got warmer, inland lakes dried up and suitable habitats became harder to find. Animals who take a long time to grow and animals with very specific needs are often the first to die out when times get tough.

It's likely that there was no single reason for the fall of the megafauna, with both environmental conditions and humans having played a role – perhaps along with another unknown cause. Hopefully future fossil discoveries will finally answer the big question – why did they disappear?

Glossary

Ambush: A surprise attack, often from a concealed position.

Amphibious: Animals that can live both on land and in water.

Archaeology: The study of past human life and culture. Archaeologists find or dig up material evidence and study it to make educated guesses about how people in the past lived.

Climate: The long-term weather patterns of a particular area.

Carnivore: An animal that primarily eats meat.

Dinosaur: A diverse group of reptiles that were dominant during the Mesozoic Era. Although most died out at the end of the Cretaceous Period, a small group of winged dinosaurs are still alive today – we call them birds!

Dreaming: An Aboriginal system of beliefs in which spiritual ancestors created the world. It is not an idea that can be fully captured by the English language.

Evolve: To change gradually over time, usually in response to environmental changes or threats.

Extinct: No surviving members of the species remain.

Family: A scientific category for classifying living things. It ranks above genus and below order.

Fossil: Preserved remains or the impression of remains of a prehistoric plant or animal.

Genus: A scientific category for classifying living things. It ranks above species and below family.

Great Ice Age: A time during the late Pleistocene Epoch when glaciers covered parts of Canada, North and South America, and northern Eurasia. Despite being cold, the Ice Age brought drier climates that likely led to the extinction of many megafauna.

Herbivore: An animal that primarily eats plants.

Marsupial: A sub-group of mammals that are born tiny, blind and hairless. They are typically carried in their mother's pouch and suckled there until fully grown.

Osteoderms: Bone plates in the skin of an animal that protect it from predators and the elements.

Palaeontology: The study of past life on Earth, including human, animal and plant life. Palaeontologists find and study fossils to make educated guesses about what life and the environment used to be like.

Predator: An animal that hunts and kills other animals to eat.

Prey: An animal that is hunted by others as a food source.

Quadrupedal: An animal that uses four limbs to move around. This could be four legs, like a horse, or two arms and two legs, like some monkeys.

Species: A group of living things capable of exchanging genes or interbreeding.

Supercontinent: A landmass made up of most or all of Earth's land. Supercontinents like Pangaea and Gondwana existed at different points in history but have since broken apart.

Hackett's Giant Echidna
(Murrayglossus hacketti)
1m long

Riversleigh Platypus
(Obdurodon dicksoni)
Up to 1m long

Newton's Thunder Bird
(Genyornis newtoni)
Over 2m tall

Marsupial Lion
(Thylacoleo carnifex)
Up to 1.5m long

Marsupial Tapir
(Palorchestes azael)
2m long

Marsupial Pygmy Hippopotamus
(Zygomaturus trilobus)
1.5m tall, 2m long

Quinkana
(Quinkana fortirostrum)
3-7m long

Average adult female
(Homo sapiens)
1.62m tall